HELEN FOGWILL PORTER has been publishing articles, stories, plays and poems for six decades. Born and raised in St. John's, she also contributed as a teacher, political activist and feminist. She has received many awards, including an honorary doctorate from Memorial University and the Order of Canada. She now lives in Paradise, Newfoundland and Labrador, where she continues to write.

"Share my crumbs!
Every poem
is a sort of Alleluia."

from "At a Poetry Reading on Holy Thursday"
by Geraldine Chafe Rubia

Full Circle

Helen Fogwill Porter

BREAKWATER

P.O. BOX 2188, ST. JOHN'S, NL, CANADA, A1C 6E6
WWW.BREAKWATERBOOKS.COM

ISBN 978-1-55081-713-3

A CIP CATALOGUE RECORD FOR THIS BOOK IS AVAILABLE FROM LIBRARY AND ARCHIVES CANADA

We acknowledge the support of the Canada Council for the Arts, which last year invested $157 million to bring the arts to Canadians throughout the country. We acknowledge the financial support of the Government of Canada through the Canada Book Fund (CBF) and the Government of Newfoundland and Labrador through the Department of Tourism, Culture and Recreation for our publishing activities.

Canada Council for the Arts | Conseil des Arts du Canada

Newfoundland Labrador

Breakwater Books is committed to choosing papers and materials for our books that help to protect our environment. To this end, this book is printed on a recycled paper that is certified by the Forest Stewardship Council®.

For my daughters, Kathy and Anne,
and my son Steve, and to the memory of
my husband, John Knight Porter, and my son,
John Robert Porter (Johnny)

Before the Fall

A Woman's Work

Full Circle

Before the Fall

Circle Game

After I wet my bed
she made them form a circle
with me in the middle
and she began to beat me

when I could no longer stand
she ordered two of the girls
to hold me up

she kept on hitting me
until she'd had enough

I was seven years old
she was a Sister of Mercy

Orange Papers

They came in wooden boxes
loosely wrapping oranges
absorbing their sweet smell

thin and delicate
they survived a long sea voyage
to reach my open hands

I liked to touch them
flatten them with my fingers
smooth them out one by one
and store them in the sideboard
to sniff and handle
on all the days when there'd be
no oranges

The Fall of a Man

Though I watched him fall
I could hardly believe
it was happening
he swayed, stood up,
and then he swayed again.
When he fell it was straight down
fast.
I could hear the crunch when his head
struck the concrete.
"Sidewalks don't care what hits them,"
a spectator remarked.

The young man who went to help him
didn't seem to be quite sure
what he should do.
Before long a crowd had gathered,
all telling each other what they thought
ought to be done.
Somebody called an ambulance
and all this time he lay on the sidewalk,
not moving,
not moving at all.

When I got on my bus
a woman who was watching
through the window
asked indignantly

why someone didn't *do* something
for the poor man.
"Everything like this affects me," she sighed.
"It seems like lately, whenever I go out
something always happens
to upset my day."

A Cure for Pessimism

My uncle Irving
a sombre man most of his life
became almost cheerful
when told he had
a fatal disease.

It was as though
he realized
that all the ghastly things
he'd been dreading for years
couldn't happen to him now
because there wouldn't
be time.

Edith

My aunt died last week.
She was old and had been sick for a long time.
It's better this way, they said, but the daughters cried
and the sons said nothing.

I could not, of course, remember her young.
She was forty-five when I was born.
Auntie, she had always been to me,
but her name was Edith.

I looked at her secret face
and smelled the flowers
she always liked flowers.
Then I sat in the church and the organ lulled me.

But something made me remember
an old man I met on the bus one day
who asked me about my people
as old men will.

He listened, nodding approval,
glad he could place me in his shrinking world
and then, as he was leaving,
he turned and said:

"The next time you sees Ede Ebsary
tell her Tom Hayes was askin about her.
She was a lovely-lookin girl
all there for a bit of fun."

The preacher announced the hymn and
I thought of Edith,
not Auntie or Mother or Nan.
I never did tell her because she was very deaf
and she probably wouldn't have heard me.

Shock Treatment

On the Maximum Security Ward
the people I met
didn't look very different
from those I see every day.
One boy had a black eye
and another had bandages
like stiff white cuffs
around both wrists
but apart from that
they looked very much like
you and me.
The boy told me he'd been
getting treatment
off and on since he was twelve.
He's twenty now.
He was moved to the ward
because he hit a nurse
who, as he put it,
was always tormenting him.
(He got the black eye
from another patient.)
My friend was there
because he threatened
to kill a man
who somehow got mixed up
with the man in his head
who wanted to do

evil things to him.

The orderly unlocked the door
to let us in
and then locked it again
behind us.

The patients sat in
a bright yellow room
but they had to signal to the orderly
when they wanted to go
to the bathroom
or anywhere else.
Most of them, I was told,
were put there for their
own protection
or the protection of others.

I turned again to the boy
with the black eye
who told me he was looking forward
to his next
shock treatment.

Inflation

Yesterday
we paid twenty dollars each
for Sunday brunch
and talked of social problems
while in the background
musicians played Bach.

Tonight
we paid thirty dollars each
for dinner
and spoke of the
materialistic age
we live in.

Tomorrow
I'll write to my foster child
in the Philippines
to say I can't afford
the bike he wants.
Poor child, he thinks Canadians
are all wealthy.
Heaven knows what he'll be
asking for
next.

Sound Poets

The other night I heard two sound poets
from London, England,
do their thing in Halifax.
They paced and shouted
shouted and paced
starting off with a kind of
latter-day Gregorian chant
and finishing with something that
sounded like a cross between
two tigers with sore throats
and a washing-machine gone wrong.

We all clapped loudly
but afterwards we asked each other
what it was all about
speaking softly for fear of being thought
behind the times.

Later on, when the poets told us
this was their fourth Canadian trip
all expenses paid
that they were going to Texas
and New Mexico
and then to Italy and Spain
I realized that they were very
sound poets indeed.

Limited Liability

Written in the early 1980s

The President talks of a limited war
A small use of nuclear power.
"Don't worry about it, we won't go too far
It should take much less than an hour."

"We must show those Commies just who is the boss
For the sake of Our Glorious Flag.
In this Land of Freedom we'll suffer no loss
We've got the whole thing in the bag."

Some people cheer but others look glum
As the movie star pauses for breath.
They know that a limited nuclear scrum
Is the same as a limited death.

Mea Culpa

He talked with authority
about the proper use of stress
suggesting that one way to combat
the negative kind
was to hire a cleaning woman
(he didn't mention the cleaning woman's stress).

"Ninety percent of people in the graveyard
are there because of poor stress handling,"
he said.
He obviously felt death
was an avoidable nuisance.

Yesterday he died of a heart attack
just stopped breathing while taking
a power nap
at a red light.
Tomorrow he'll join the others
in the cemetery
stressed out and stressless
lying side by side.

Sunday Best

It's Sunday and I'm washing the dishes
from my late lonely lunch.
The sharp tap on the door startles me.
Standing there is a young man
in Salvation Army uniform
with a bundle of *War Crys* under his arm.

"Mrs. Porter?" he asks, smiling,
and my heart sinks.
It's a visit then, not a drop-off.
I show him into the living room
conscious of my shabby jeans
and the blob of mustard on my blouse.

As he settles himself I remember
long-ago Sundays when wearing jeans
would seem a kind of sin.
I hunch my shoulders to hide
the mustard smear.

"I'm Cadet Carter," he says, still smiling.
His teeth gleam white, he has a small mustache.
"I've been asked to call on you now and then
along with others we don't see in church very often."

I know if I open my mouth
I'll make a fool of myself
but that doesn't stop me.
"Oh, I still go to church sometimes," I splutter.

"My daughter goes to Gower and I go with her."
I try hard to remember the last time
either of us was there.

He smiles wider and says
"Well, as long as you go somewhere."
I find myself nodding and smiling back.
Why can't I tell him I'm not a believer
that I don't think there's any heaven
or any hell either, except the one on earth,
and ask him why God's son had to die on a cross
to save us from sins we had not yet committed?

As if he sees into my mind
he turns in his Bible to Psalm 51
and reads in a clear persuasive voice
"Behold, I was shapen in iniquity
and in sin did my mother conceive me.
Purge me with hyssop, and I shall be clean.
Wash me, and I shall be whiter than snow."
As I listen I think of my grandchildren.
I cannot see them as such deep-dyed sinners.
Does this man really believe what he's reading?

He kneels on the floor to pray
and I bow my head.
He murmurs words about family and love and blood.
I'm no longer concerned about the stain
on my shirt.

Before he leaves he tells me
he might not get back to see me for a while.
I try not to show my relief.
He opens his notebook and points to a list of names.
My fellow sinners.
"I don't have a car," he says,
"so I do one neighbourhood each Sunday."

When I close the door I want to weep
but I don't know why.
Is it because I've lost my faith?
Or because I'm remembering the Sundays
of long ago
when we all went to my mother's after church
and ate the kind of dinner only she could cook?
Or do I weep for this young man
so secure in his salvation that he gives his life
to the cause
and trudges from house to house on Sundays
bringing the good news of the gospel
to people like me?

On Our Street

A song

We're a high-class band of people from a
high-class part of town
And we get along together very well.
Our lawns are all clipped neatly and our
weeds are all kept down
And our floors are spick and spotless, you can tell.
But when we heard about the Crazies that were
moving in
We were scared to death, our hearts all skipped
a beat.
We'd love for them to have a home outside the
looney-bin
But for God's sake please don't put them
on our street.

On our street, on our street
Oh for God's sake please don't put them
on our street
You can drop them anywhere, in a Circle,
Court or Square
But for God's sake please don't put them
on our street.

We work hard for our money, we deserve a decent life
For ourselves and for our children too, of course.
We're law-abiding citizens, we don't want any strife.
If we have to we'll remove that crowd by force.

We feel for them sincerely, we wish they had a home
But we have to keep our money values sweet.
Surely downtown would be better for where they're
        coming from;
We don't see why we should have them on our street.

    On our street, on our street
    Oh for God's sake please don't put them
        on our street
    You can drop them anywhere, in a Circle,
        Court or Square
    But for God's sake please don't put them
        on our street.

One winter many years ago a young man came along
Just like this gang he was searching for a bed.
He looked at us so strangely and he sang a scary song
About love and peace and rising from the dead;
His clothes were torn and shabby, he didn't smell too
        good
And oh my God, you should have seen his feet!
We hope he found some shelter, you know we're never
        rude
But we really couldn't have him on our street.

    On our street, on our street
    No, we really couldn't have Him on our street
    You can drop Him anywhere, in a Stable,
        Court or Square
    But for Christ's sake please don't put Him
        on our street.

Conversion

It used to be a place
where souls were saved
or so they claimed. "Have you been
to Jesus for the cleansing power?"
they used to ask.
"Are you washed in the Blood of the Lamb?"

Drunkards knelt
and the congregation, behind their hands,
wondered if the poor souls
knew what they were doing.
Some of them held on,
testifying often in clichés
(probably sincere, for all that)
to God's saving and keeping power
and the chain-breaking ability
of the Lion of Judah.

Sometimes, not lately but years ago,
those converts sang a warning
about the swearer
and the drunkard
"and the man who had sold him the drink."
Today the building wears another face,
all fancy angel-stone and pastel paint.
The old men have died,
some of them still sober,
and the new Brewer's Retail practises
a different kind of conversion.

A Woman's Work

A Woman's Work

Masonic Park Nursing Home, Mount Pearl, c. 1985

Mary is scrubbing again, her practiced hands,
half-clenched, move back and forth
across the smooth surface.
She looks up and says: "Don't you track mud
over my clean floor," but then
her green eyes light up with that leprechaun grin
and she asks for a cigarette.
"Busy today?" I say as she takes
short happy puffs.
"Don't be talkin. I never stopped a minute,
had to mix the bread and wash the quilts
and you shoulda seen the ironing.
I had a job to keep the fire goin."
She finishes the cigarette and begins
to scrub once more.
A nurse comes by, straightens the strap
around Mary's waist and says,
"Time for bed now, my love."
As the nurse pushes the wheelchair
down the hall, Mary turns to wink at me
as if she and I are the only ones
who really know what's going on.

Evensong

for Peter Miller

"Cheer up, the weekend's almost here"
"Thank the Lord it's Friday!"
Why should I pray for Saturday?
I know it won't be my day.

Snacks in odd corners, grimy plates
And constant bathroom clashes.
Too much to do—I can't get through
This haze of dust and ashes.

Then, when the boys go out at night
They won't say where they're going;
I swallow pills to warm my chills
And keep my fears from growing.

The sound of church bells, buried guilt,
The sombre sprawl of Sunday.
By night I feel compelled to kneel
And thank the Lord for Monday.

The Shovellers

When I was a little girl
I often heard my father say
when he was talking to his union friends
about rotten working conditions:
"I'd rather be shovelling shit."
Shovelling shit was, of course,
the ultimate indignity;
I suppose it still is
though there's not as much of it now,
at least not from horses.

Poor Dad, I don't suppose he ever realized
(kind man that he is)
that shovelling shit is something
women are expected to do
as a matter of course.
The first time I did it
the shit belonged to a baby,
my own baby, which is supposed to make it
a little easier.
I did it often for the next few years
putting up with the way I felt about it
because if I didn't do it
who would?

Since then I've done it
for an old woman

and I'll probably have to do it
again.

Perhaps one day I'll ask my father
if there's a union for
people like me
and if so
how much do we have to shovel
to qualify?

Lament from the Laundry Room

I just had an idea for a poem
but now I've forgotten it—
oh well, what does it matter?
It probably wouldn't have been
a very good one.

I think it was something
about how I can't attempt
a novel
because it just seems too big,
my writing has to be all

bits
and
pieces

I wonder why that is?

Oh Lord, it's five o'clock already
and I've got to make scruncheons
and drawn butter
for the salt fish.

I still can't remember
what I was going to write—
perhaps it will come back to me later
when I come down
to fold the towels.

Streel in Waiting

From The Dictionary of Newfoundland English*: "Streel (verb): To drag along the ground, to haul or hang untidily. Streelish, also streely: Of a woman, untidy, slatternly in appearance."*

I grew up believing it was wrong
to let yourself go
(go where?)
women especially were warned against this
all kinds of consequences could follow
like losing
        your looks
            your husband
                your self-respect

but now I think often
how wonderful it
would be
to do just that
let myself go.

        I read somewhere
        that people are more likely
        to shower every day
        than to use condoms when they have sex.

Cleanliness is next to godliness
has become
cleanliness instead of godliness.
It's one of the few precepts we have left.

Would you rather someone said of you
she's dishonest,
he's mean
or
she's a streel,
he smells?
Think about it.

"It's easier to be dirty than clean,"
my mother used to say
quoting her mother
when she heard women criticized
for being lousy housekeepers—
or just plain lousy.

"There's always a little drop of water,"
the virtuously clean claim,
"There's always a little bit of soap."

What gave total immersion its high status?
Are baths and showers a replacement for baptism
or being Washed in the Blood of the Lamb,
which by some weird process
made you whiter than snow?

Old people are urged
to keep themselves clean
(if you want others to love you
is the unspoken refrain).

Mad people often refuse to wash
(some say the mad
are the only truly sane).

Poets have written of what they'll do
when they quit their day jobs:
wear purple hats,
let their hair grow grey and wild,
shout what's on their minds.
I haven't heard one of them
vow to stop bathing.
Surely I won't be the first?

The New If

If you can keep your hair when all about you
Are tearing theirs, and blaming it on you;
If you can keep your cool when others doubt you
Yet let them know that doubts are valid, too;
If you stay calm when journalists attack you
Because you dare to question status quo;
If you can smile when commentators hack you
But yet speak up, and tell them where to go.

If you hear one more reference to bra burning
And resist the urge to knock the speaker cold;
If it's for true equality you're yearning,
If you try hard to break the man-made mould;
If you can stay good friends with all your sisters
Though they don't always see things as you do;
If you refuse to join with the desisters
Who sit on fences, scared of something new

If you refuse to stay as sweet as honey
When putdowns from the jocks make your blood boil;
If you don't think that sexism is funny,
If from sick humour you have to recoil;
If you speak out, although you're tempted not to,
If you just will not play the old male game;
If you recall where compromise had got you,
If you refuse to shoulder all the blame

If you can keep up steam, and not get weary,
Although at times the struggle seems too hard;
Relax, bounce back, not daunted, or not very,
Although it's tempting to let down your guard;
If you reject that Total Woman fibber
(Who knows that what she's saying is not true);
Well then, my maid, you'll be a Women's Libber,
And, what is more, a Real Strong Woman, too.

The Crossroads of the World

In memory of Clara, 1904-1963

Gazing at a lighted candle
inside a lamp chimney
at the Albatross Hotel in Gander
in 1985,
I let my thoughts slip back
to long before the War
when there was no Albatross Hotel,
indeed no Gander
just a tiny spot on the railroad
called the Newfoundland Airport
that we used to pass
on our way to Notre Dame Junction.

I thought of the women who lived
near here at that time
whose lamp chimneys were not for decoration
but to cover a flame
that lit a child to bed
and then burned brightly in the hall
to keep away the boogyman.

They didn't travel, those women,
their men went to sea
but they stayed home

to light the lamps
and clean the chimneys,
to make fish on the flakes
while the sun shone and
walk a mile to their gardens
to take a spell.

If I could meet one of those women now
across a table lighted by an oil lamp
what would I have to say to her
or she to me?

Food for Thought

for Pauline

When I'm travelling on the CN bus
how can I possibly resist
the turkey and chips with gravy
at the Corner Book terminal
or the double-decker ice-cream at
Robinson's
where the cones have the full
flavour of much-fried fat?

At Baie Verte junction
I linger to buy a Sweet Marie
and then realize in panic
that the bus is gone.
The driver backs up when he sees me
running, not wanting a heart attack
victim on his record.
In Gander I look longingly at the
roast pork with apple sauce
but settle instead for the bacon burger
for fear of being left behind again.
The driver might not be so understanding
a second time.
At the last second I grab a chocolate doughnut
to munch on the bus.

In Clarenville I buy a Pal-o-Mine.
It reminds me of summer Sundays
in Bowring Park when chocolate bars
cost six cents
(five before the war).

When I get home, Pauline has a hot supper
ready for me
which I refuse to eat
reminding her reproachfully
that I'll never reach my ideal weight
unless she co-operates.

Wild People

On Saturday nights when we were twelve
Dot and I would wangle a few dollars from
    our grandfather
enough to buy ice-cream sodas and homemade candy
at Powers' Store on New Gower Street
or if we were daring,
chips and vinegar across the street at the People's Cafe
with its oilclothed tables and yellow unshaded lights.

In the forties, none of the Chinese restaurants
had Chinese names.
Sometimes their windows advertised
Chop Suey or Chow Mein
but nobody ever bought any
as far as I know. We grew up believing that Chinese food
was fish and chips.

Mom and Aunt Daisy warned us not to go
to the People's Cafe.
They never went there themselves
preferring the Mayfair or the Sweet Shoppe,
which were run by respectable white businessmen.
"The People's Cafe is dirty," they said,
"and you never know what might happen there."
Of course we kept going
shivering each time with the fear of being found out.
We asked for chips wrapped in brown paper
so that we could take off at the first sign of trouble
and finish our feast as we strolled.

One night when we got to Bairds' Department Store
our fingers were stinking of vinegar.
Mary Power sniffed and asked, "Where'd you get the
    chips?
You're makin me hungry."
Mary served behind the counter at Bairds'
and lived on our street.
We swore her to secrecy.

Once at People's we weren't fast enough
and the fight started while we were still there.
Two American sailors shouted across a table
and then began to punch each other out.
The girls with them moved closer together
their impossibly golden heads almost touching.

"They're two bad ones," Dot whispered.
"'Member we saw them at the Station that time?"
Mom and Aunt Daisy always pulled us away
when we came close to girls like that.
Streetwalkers, they called them
and pitied the men who picked them up.

The proprietor spoke sharply to the sailors.
"Shut up, Chink!" yelled one of them.
"You can't even speak English right."
And "Chinky chinky Chineeman/Belly full of rats,"
roared the other. The fight was over.

There were lots of Chinese men in St. John's
but no Chinese women.
The only children were the ones Aunt Daisy
called half-breeds,
products of Chinese/Newfoundland unions.
Hard tickets, they were called.

Sometimes when I picked up my father's shirts at
Kim Lee Laundry
I peeped through the curtains at the half-naked men
sweating over wash-tubs in the steamy inside room.
Most of them had wives in China, Mom told me.
They saw them maybe once in twenty years.
"Why can't the women come here?" I asked,
"Those men must be very lonely."
"They'd breed and overrun us," Aunt Daisy said.
"Anyway, they don't have feelings like we do."

The night of the fight we finally escaped
with our precious paper packages.
As we left the Café, the owner was standing
in the doorway
smoking a cigarette.
He smiled sadly as we shrank away from him
and ran down the street.

"Mom says the Chinese are wild people,"
said Dot. "You got to watch out for them."

To My Son

When you were small
you used to climb
into our bed
when lightning ripped the sky.
We'd hold you tight
between us
while your father said,
"That storm is miles away,"
a second before the room
was lit
with fearsome light.

Now when lightning strikes
you stay in your own
narrow bed
trying to think of other
safer things
and we in our wide bed
sigh separate sighs
because we no longer know how
to comfort you.

Unpardonable Sin

There's only one thing
I cannot forgive you for—
the guilt I carry.

Full Circle

Full Circle

When Joan was two her mother
Pushed her down the cellar stairs;
When Joan was four her father left
As he'd planned to do for years.

When Joan was five she went to school
The teacher said, "My, my
Your work is very poor, Joan,
But you'll really have to try."

"Oh, Joan, you're such a dirty child,
Your blouse is soiled and torn;
Your nails are black, your nose, oh dear,"
And she turned away in scorn.

When Joan was eight the children laughed
And called her "Stinky Joan"
They held their nose when she passed by
And doused her with cologne.

When Joan was ten she went to church
Just wandered in one day;
The preacher had a kindly face
When he chanted, "Let us pray."

He shook her hand and pinched her cheek,
Said, "How are you, my dear?
Why don't you come to Sunday School?
I'm sure you'd like it there."

In Sunday School she heard about
Frail Jesus on the tree;
And Joseph's coat, and Peter's cross,
And Immortality.

But when the Christmas concert came
The Easter Pageant, too,
The teacher said, "I'm sorry, Joan,
I have no part for you."

In school Joan failed another year.
The teacher shook his head;
Her mother said, "You stupid slut!"
And beat her till she bled.

The boys still followed her, but now
To kiss and hug and squeeze;
And when they wanted something more
Joan tried so hard to please.

She wore her sweater very tight
And shortened up her skirt
And put her mother's makeup on
And smiled until it hurt.

She left the school and went to work
In a factory packing fish.
Men looked, and nudged, and looked again
And said "She's quite a dish."

But then a sailor came along
And stole her heart away.
Her mother made him marry Joan
One rainy August day.

When Joan was only seventeen
She had a baby girl;
Her eyes were blue, her cheeks were soft
Her daddy named her Pearl.

When Pearl was four, her mother
Pushed her down the cellar stairs;
When Pearl was six her father left
As he'd planned to do for years.

The Remedy

"I only had one sister,"
said the old woman
at the Agnes Pratt Home
"and she died when she was
seventeen.
Six brothers, but you know brothers
are not the same.
They're all dead now.
Hazel, that was my sister's name,
Hazel was a pretty girl,
she had black hair
right down her back.
Some people said that's
what happened to her,
her strength went out
in her hair.
She was fifteen when she
got sick. Consumption,
the old people called it then.
She had a dreadful cough,
that used to keep her awake
all night long
and me, too, because
I slept with her.
We didn't know it was
catching.
I remember
when she started to take

the medicine.
Mother had bought it
from a student minister
who told her he'd made it
himself
and that it was a sure cure
for lung trouble.
Mother believed him because
after all he was a Man of God
and she knew he wouldn't
lie.
For a while Hazel seemed
to be getting better
and Mom kept buying
more medicine.
She couldn't really afford it,
times were hard
in those days
but nothing was too good
for her children.
After a while it didn't matter
how much of the remedy
she took
Hazel just kept coughing
more and more.
She was so thin you could
see through her
and her cheeks were as red
as if they'd

been dyed.
I was with her
the night it happened
she couldn't stop coughing
and then the blood came.
She'd haemorrhaged before
but never like this.
When it was over
she was dead.
Mom laid her out
herself
in a beautiful blue dress
that one of our cousins
had sent from the States
but when Father said
he was going after
the young man
who sold the medicine
to ask him to conduct
the funeral
Mom screamed at him
that he was to do
no such thing.
She went herself to the
other clergyman
the one from the church
across the harbour
the strange church that
people said

only the scroff went to.
She got him to come
for the funeral
and everyone wondered
why.
I've heard since that
the student minister
became a famous poet
but whenever I hear his name
I remember my sister's
cough
that no amount of his
remedy
could stop.
I'm glad it was
the other minister
who said the words
over her."

Easy Prey

For Alice Wood, 1927-1995

I stand on the edge waiting
for the predators to pause.
When they shudder and stop
I move forward,
eyes and ears taut

the haven I reach is temporary.

My heart hits my ribs
as I assess my chances,
step out again

Fiery eyes stare savagely
and too late I hear
the reverberating roar.

Hot Night in July

In St. John's Centre on sultry nights like this we sit on our doorsteps and chat with our neighbours. One old man wanders from house to house, trying to remember what he's looking for. My old black tomcat wakes from a dream of his hedonistic prime; he fixes his gaze on the young tabby across the street and slowly saunters over.

"Beautiful night," I say to the man next door. "Fantastic," he replies, smiling. He looks good in his khaki shorts, firm and strong and limber. He has no wife, I have no husband. Why are we always so polite?

I stroll along the sidewalk with no destination. Rock music blares from the open windows. Teenagers stride by, six-packs cradled in their arms. They do not see me.

The sweet smell of mock orange mingles with fabric softener from the laundromat. Fat fries out Leo's back window. In a nearby doorway an old woman with wild white hair wheedles "The Star of Logy Bay" from her mouth organ while her daughter paints the window trim, paying no attention to the lowering light. Through his open door the shopkeeper on the corner hands a dripping popsicle to a passing child. She grabs it quickly and hurries away, afraid he might change his mind.

On LeMarchant Road a taxi driver snuggles with his sweetheart in the back seat of his Chevrolet while the intercom transmits unheeded instructions. At Caul's Funeral Home there are no cars in the parking lots.

When I wander reluctantly back to my house, my neighbour is still sitting on his steps whistling at the moon. He interrupts himself to bid me good-night.

In my bedroom I kneel at the open window, an elderly Juliet.

Mrs. Brown

She walks
from room to room
searching hard for something
that can only be found
in museums.

Proper Dress

I don't worry too much about fashion
but last week I found myself wondering
about the proper apparel
to wear to a poetry reading.

The poet herself, who would be the first
to tell you she couldn't care less about clothes,
was wearing a loose embroidered cotton dress
with thick black boots just visible beneath.

I looked down, alarmed, at my own brown pantsuit,
comfortable, to be sure, but polyester?
Hastily I tucked my feet away
to hide the wedgies and the nylon knee-highs.

The room was full of denim and hand weaving
and boots a trapper would have found too warm.
Surrounded so by people spurning fashion,
I sat, self-conscious, stiff and out of style.

Middle-Aged Radical at a Poetry Reading

And he rails on bitterly
against the obscene forces
that pollute the land
and befoul the sea
and destroy the air
and all the while he
sucks hungrily on his
cigarette
and putrefies
the atmosphere.

Passed Away

Yesterday I went to Mrs. Mercer's funeral
This morning I heard that Dave Burton
was found dead in his bathroom
(no visitation, thank God)
Theresa just phoned to tell me
Larry Taylor had "passed away"
she gave me the visiting times
and the funeral hour
I didn't ask her.

I cancelled the *Telegram*
because I didn't want to know all this
but someone always tells me.

For every death there's a network
                        stretching across town
                                    across the country
                                                across the world,
reaching those of us
who'd rather not be reached.

Mrs. Mercer had Alzheimer's.
I've never been able to think of anything good
about having Alzheimer's
but she was spared the knowledge
of a lot of deaths
including
her own.

The Dancer

I never expected to feel like this
at my age. I thought by this time I'd be
calm and serene,
occupied by things like gourmet recipes
and refinishing old tables.

Instead it's like I'm seventeen again.
March flashes through my flesh as it did then,
leaving me weak and warm and wondering
what happens next? Will people think I'm strange
with my hair long and straight, though streaking grey?

Why can't I reconcile myself to proper dresses
and hairdos more becoming to my age?
My mother did, and lived in peace.
Or did she? I can't believe she ever felt
as I do now, but how would I know?

My daughters think I'm sensible and solid,
someone who's always there to call them
        in the morning,
to cook the roast and order pants from Eaton's.
What would they say, I wonder, if I told them
I'd like to go play marbles in the mud?

Or waltz around the kitchen while a country singer
warbles about falling to pieces—is that what I'm doing?
I never was much of a dancer, although
I always wanted to be. Maybe that
or something else is what's wrong with me now.

The Series

With thanks to Steve O'Brien and Steve Porter

SPRING 1997

Looking up a number in the phone book
I come across your name.
There it is on Page 262:
G. Whitty Calver Street.

FALL 1954

In your office at the Justice Department
across the hall from mine
we listened to the World Series
on the radio you smuggled in.
Later I caught hell from Miss Bartlett
for not being where I was supposed to be
when she came prowling.

Was that the year Willie Mays became
the Dodgers' hitting star?

You told me all about The Dizzy Dean Story,
the only movie you'd seen in years—
you watched it four times.

The Brooklyn Dodgers were soon
my team too
though I'd hardly heard of them
before that summer.
They fitted the ordinary guy image
that was so much a part of St. John's
and of you.

You organized your bookkeeping
without missing an out
Mr. Howley turned his hearing aid off
while he worked.
He didn't follow baseball.

Spring 1997

They tell me you're at the Miller Centre,
that if I went to visit
you wouldn't know me
You've forgotten Roy Campanella,
Pee Wee Reese
and even Jackie Robinson

but there's your name leaping out
at me
I want to dial the number—
instead I stare at the page
and think of Ebbets Field.

The Lady Vanishes

I used to measure five foot six
when I was young and spry.
Today I measure five foot two
O Lord I want to cry.

Where did those four rogue inches go?
Can't find them anywhere.
Perhaps if I live long enough
I'll simply disappear.

No need for hot cremation then,
no funeral bills to pay.
I'll slowly crumble into dust
and softly steal away.